Agentic

Building Smarter, Autonomous Systems for the Future of Work and Innovation

Jaxon Vale

DEDICATION

This book is dedicated to everyone who has the audacity to envision a time when technology and mankind live side by side in harmony and where artificial and human intelligence collaborate to create a better world. May the efforts of the innovators, philosophers, and visionaries who are reshaping the future inspire and lead us to a time characterized by cooperation, compassion, and advancement.

To my mentors, family, and friends—who have been my beacon of hope with their unfailing encouragement, support, and faith in the potential of all people. Every stage of this trip has been important because of you.

Lastly, I would like to wish that this book would inspire and empower readers as we all work together to navigate the future. As we continue to push the limits of knowledge and technology, may we never lose sight of the principles that define who we are as humans.

DISCLAIMER

This book's content is solely intended for educational and informational purposes. Current knowledge, research, and individual insights at the time of writing form the basis of the ideas, thoughts, and viewpoints presented. Although every attempt has been taken to guarantee the quality and dependability of the material supplied, certain elements may become out-of-date or subject to change due to the quick evolution of artificial intelligence and technology.

Any liability or responsibility for any mistakes or omissions, or for any consequences resulting from the use of this information, is disclaimed by the author, publisher, and any affiliates. Before making any judgments based on the information in this book, the reader is urged to carry out additional study and speak with pertinent authorities or experts.

The opinions presented in this book are those of the author and may not represent those of any institution, organization, or other entity that is connected to the author.

You understand and accept the conditions of this disclaimer

by reading this book.

CONTENTS

ACKNOWLEDGMENTS

I want to sincerely thank everyone who has helped me along the way as I've been writing this book. This work would not have been possible without the assistance, support, and knowledge of numerous people.

Thank you for your undying love, patience, and understanding, family, who have been my pillar of support and belief in my mission. Throughout the process, your support has been a beacon of hope, and I will always be thankful that you are in my life.

To the colleagues, mentors, and specialists in the domains of artificial intelligence, technology, and ethics, your experience and insights have considerably enriched this book. Your readiness to impart your expertise and participate in meaningful dialogues has greatly influenced the concepts covered in these pages.

My editor and the whole publishing team deserve special recognition. Your professionalism, careful attention to detail, and insightful criticism have made sure that this work is of the greatest caliber. You have played a crucial role in turning my idea into a completed piece.

Last but not least, I want to thank the readers for their interest and curiosity, which drive me to keep researching and disseminating new concepts. I hope this book adds something significant to your knowledge about agentic AI and how it could change the world.

I want to express my sincere gratitude to everyone who has contributed to this journey.

CHAPTER 1

THE EMERGENCE OF AGENTIC AI

1.1 Artificial Intelligence's Development: From Rule-Based to Autonomous Systems

We must first look at the development of artificial intelligence in order to comprehend the birth of agentic AI. For many years, a wide range of computing abilities, some incredibly brilliant, others deceptively mechanical have been referred to as artificial intelligence (AI). The evolution of intelligent, self-directed agents from early rule-based programs to the present day represents both a paradigm shift in how machines interact with the outside world and technological improvement.

Beginnings Based on Rules

The first artificial intelligence systems were rule-bound and deterministic. Popular from the 1960s to the 1980s, these expert systems used if-then logic:

2

- Take action B if condition A is true.
- Decisions lacked complexity and were preprogrammed.
- These systems performed well in specialized fields like tax preparation or medical diagnosis (e.g., MYCIN), but they struggled in dynamic, unclear settings.

There was no generalization in rule-based systems. They were fragile, breaking down when faced with unexpected input. They simply carried out what people programmed into them; they didn't learn.

Machine Learning's Inception

- With the introduction of machine learning (ML) in the late 1990s and early 2000s, artificial intelligence underwent a dramatic change. Machine learning (ML) systems could examine data and spot trends, enabling machines to "learn" from examples:
- Algorithms like neural networks, support vector machines, and decision trees became popular.
- Systems were not merely programmed; they were

trained.

- Though still not perfect, AI's ability to generalize outside of its training data is increasing.

This was the beginning of statistical learning and eventually deep learning, which made it possible to recognize voice, classify images, and comprehend natural language.

Systems Transitioning from Reactive to Adaptive

- AI evolved from reactive behavior to increasingly adaptive systems as ML and deep learning advanced:
- On tasks involving language and picture categorization, deep neural networks started to surpass humans.
- Reinforcement learning hinted at early goal-directed systems by introducing reward-driven behavior.

Nevertheless, agency was lacking. These systems needed human guidance and assistance despite their strength. They lacked autonomy, long-term planning, and the capacity to establish and follow objectives on their own.

This puts us on the cusp of a new era agentic AI in which systems start acting intentionally, autonomously, and contextually in response to changing objectives, rather than merely learning from data.

1.2 Agentic AI: What Is It Different?

A new generation of AI systems known as agentic AI operate as agents entities that are able to sense their surroundings, set objectives, make decisions, and behave purposefully instead of being static tools.

Essential Features of Agentic AI

Understanding the characteristics that set agentic AI apart from classical AI is essential:

- Autonomy: Agentic systems are capable of functioning autonomously and reaching judgments without the assistance of humans. They modify their course of action in response to shifting circumstances and internal success assessments.

- Goal-Orientation: Agentic AI is motivated by objectives as opposed to reactive systems. In order to achieve a desired end-state, such as resolving an issue, improving a system, or helping a human, it plans, carries out, and reassesses steps.

- Adaptability: These agents are not restricted to a particular use case or environment. They learn in real time and develop via interaction, honing their tactics as circumstances shift.

- Self-Directed Learning: Meta-learning or learning to learn is a common feature of agentic AI. Without direct human retraining, it may change its behavior, seek out new information, and revise its knowledge.

- Interactivity: These systems are made to work together. They can negotiate tasks, interact with people or other machines, and even modify their behavior in response to organizational or social dynamics.

How It Modifies the Connection to Technology

The conventional paradigm, in which people issue commands and machines follow them, is called into question by agentic AI. Such systems function more like colleagues or collaborators instead:

- They offer fresh ideas, improve assignments, or even caution against unforeseen repercussions.
- They can be given a broad objective (such as "maximize customer retention") and investigate various approaches to achieve it.

This degree of initiative represents a significant advancement a computer that knows what to do* and understands why it matters.

1.3 The Present Need for Agentic AI? Social Needs, Technological Maturity, and Timing

Agentic AI wasn't created overnight. The emergence of this new class of intelligent systems is the consequence of a number of convergent pressures, including technological, economic, and sociological ones.

Core Technology Maturity

Once experimental, many of the fundamental components of AI are now reliable and scalable:

- It is now possible to train large-scale models with billions of parameters thanks to cloud computing and GPUs.
- Experimental barriers are decreased by APIs, open-source libraries, and frameworks (e.g., PyTorch, Hugging Face).
- Transformer models (such as GPT and BERT) facilitate sophisticated language comprehension, reasoning, and problem-solving.

Long-term memory modules, planning engines, and goal arbitration are some of the technologies that support agentic behavior, and they are becoming both accessible and useful at scale.

Growth of Available Information

Large volumes of data are necessary for both interaction

and context, which are essential for agentic AI to flourish:

- The rich, contextual input required to support agentic reasoning is provided by the digitization of work, communication, and behavior.

- The complex settings in which human agents function can now be mirrored by multi-modal models, which comprehend text, images, sounds, and more.

Economic and Social Demands

Smarter, more flexible technology is required by modern society:

- Workforce transformation: Repetitive automation is no longer adequate as tasks get more complex. Dynamic adaptation, inventiveness, and decision-making can all be aided by agentic systems.

- Complex global challenges: Problems like supply chain disruption, healthcare inequality, and climate change necessitate the use of tools that can reason independently across contexts and domains.

- The expectations of the user: These days, we expect our gadgets to do more than just meet our requirements; they should anticipate them. Users want more seamless and intuitive engagement from digital assistants, self-driving cars, and business efficiency tools.

Essentially, agentic AI is not just possible now it is required.

1.4 A Comparison between Conventional Automation and Agentic AI

It's important to examine what agentic AI isn't in order to comprehend what it is. Its transformational potential is highlighted when compared to typical automation.

Conventional Automation: Effectiveness Above Cunning

- Fixed Workflow: Automation follows preset workflows and regulations. Consider robotic arms on assembly lines or scripts processing invoices as examples of its proficiency in high-volume, low-variance jobs.

- No Learning: Unless actively reprogrammed, automated systems do not adapt. Automation malfunctions or generates errors as conditions change.

- No Contextual Awareness: Conventional automation is not aware of the circumstance or the environment. Regardless of whether the work is still appropriate, it completes it.

- Reactive just: These systems don't start things or redefine tasks; they just react to triggers.

Agentic AI: Adaptive Intelligence

- Dynamic Workflow: Workflows are designed or modified in real time by agentic systems. The system adjusts if conditions change or a goal becomes outdated.

- Continuous Learning: Without outside assistance, agentic AI improves its comprehension through feedback, reinforcement, and meta-learning.

- Before taking action, context-driven behavior takes into consideration the larger environment, including user preferences, system limitations, and temporal variables.

- Proactivity: Without being specifically asked, agentic computers can start tasks, offer advice, or even warn users about possible dangers.

This difference is crucial: agentic AI thinks and decides, whereas automation executes. It is an emerging partner in problem-solving, not just a more intelligent instrument.

A turning point in the development of artificial intelligence has been reached with the emergence of agentic AI. We are now developing systems that can reason on their own, adapt to their environment, and behave pro-actively, going beyond machines that only follow rules. Their rise is a reflection of both the pressing demand for more intelligent, responsive systems in the complicated world of today and the convergence of technological maturity. Deeper investigation of agentic AI's uses, architecture, hazards, and future is made possible by an understanding of where we've been and how it differs from its predecessors.

This marks the beginning of a new form of intelligence, not merely an advancement in AI.

CHAPTER 2

THE FUNDAMENTAL IDEAS OF AGENTIC INTELLIGENCE

The emergence of agentic intelligence is a turning point in the development of artificial intelligence, a time when machines are capable of more than just computation, response, and command execution; they are also able to think strategically, adjust to changing conditions, and internalize values to act responsibly. Agentic AI systems are made to think, learn, and behave with a great deal of autonomy, in contrast to classical automation, which depends on clear instructions and predictable patterns. This chapter examines the fundamental ideas that underpin agentic intelligence and set these sentient beings apart from both traditional automation and previous AI models.

2.1 Independence and Goal-Oriented Conduct

The autonomy concept is central to agentic intelligence. A static set of rules is not all that an agentic AI adheres to.

Rather, it functions with self-determined aim, carrying out choices in accordance with more general goals that it comprehends and absorbs.

What does AI autonomy mean?

The ability of a system to function independently under challenging and frequently unclear situations is known as autonomy. Without the need for detailed instructions, an autonomous agent sees the environment, processes sensory information, and acts accordingly.

Autonomy in the context of agentic AI is more than just independence. It has its roots in deliberate action. The AI determines objectives, justifies possible courses of action, and implements plans to reach those goals.

Qualities of Goal-Directed Conduct

The skills that allow an agentic system to behave consistently and intelligently are collectively referred to as goal-directed behavior. These consist of:

- Intentionality: The AI consistently understands what it is attempting to accomplish. Although they are frequently placed within a larger objective hierarchy, goals are not arbitrary.

- Planning: The system uses world models to chart out a course of action, assessing possible outcomes and selecting routes that advance its objectives.

- The ability of agentic AI to make decisions in the face of uncertainty is a result of its ability to adapt to changing conditions. In the face of uncertainty or danger, it recalculates, reorients, and proceeds.

- Prioritization: These systems are able to optimize choices in real time by balancing conflicting goals and trade-offs.

Practical Illustration

Think about an agentic AI-powered warehouse robot. This system independently determines which items to sort depending on delivery urgency, assesses the efficiency of obstacle-filled courses, and reroutes itself when new instructions or unforeseen circumstances arise, in contrast to previous robots that followed predefined tracks and performed fixed duties. The why as well as the how of the system's operations are understood.

2.2 Adaptability and Context Awareness

Agentic systems are not isolated entities. They exist in settings that are frequently dynamic, erratic, and influenced by social interactions. An agentic AI must exhibit high levels of contextual awareness and adaptability in order to operate well in such circumstances.

Comprehending Context

The ability to recognize, understand, and incorporate outside influences into one's decision-making process is known as context awareness. These elements may consist of:

- Environmental cues, such as traffic, temperature, and location

- Temporal components (such as the time of day or the order of events)
- Social context (e.g., group dynamics, conversational tone, and human emotions)
- Historical memory (such as past encounters, results, and patterns learned)

Flexibility in Practice

The ability to adjust behavior in response to immediate input and changes in the environment is known as adaptability. In terms of agentic AI, this implies:

When inputs change, strategies should be adjusted. Routines should be interrupted to handle new situations. Knowledge should be transferred from one task or area to another. Behaviors should be changed over time to coincide with long-term success.

Systems that Facilitate Flexibility

This flexibility is supported by a number of computational techniques:

- Reinforcement Learning: The system improves behaviors based on incentives and punishments as it learns by making mistakes.
- Bayesian Inference: AI helps it adjust in uncertain situations by updating beliefs based on new evidence.
- Meta-learning ("learning to learn"): By knowing how to approach learning, the system increases its learning efficiency.

Typical Situation

Consider a virtual agent that assists with meeting scheduling. Not only does it parse calendar data, but it also recognizes the user's communication style, predicts the possibility of rescheduling based on historical behavior, and even analyzes email tone to determine the urgency of meetings. This is context-shaped responsive intelligence, not just pattern recognition.

2.3 Loops of Ongoing Learning and Reflection

The ability of agentic systems to continuously learn and get better over time is one of their defining characteristics. These agents are dynamic beings with the ability to reflect on and better themselves rather than being static stores of preprogrammed knowledge.

Ongoing Education

Agentic AI systems are made for lifelong learning, in contrast to conventional machine learning models that are trained once and then put into use. They gradually incorporate new information, modifying choices and actions without undergoing total retraining.

Among the essential elements of ongoing learning are:

- Incremental Updates: New experiences are added to the model's current body of knowledge.
- Plasticity-Stability Balance: The system avoids overfitting and forgetting by retaining prior knowledge while absorbing new patterns.
- Cross-Domain Generalization: By abstracting concepts, knowledge gained in one area improves

performance in another.

Loops of Reflection

The ability of an AI to assess its own decisions and results is known as reflection. Reflection allows the system to:

- Evaluate success and failure: Did the result match the objective?
- Find trends: Which tactics are effective? Which aren't?
- Reformulate goals: Is there a more ethical or efficient approach to accomplish the same goal?
- The internal models should be adjusted. Enhance world representations to make decisions that are more correct.

Structures that Encourage Introspection

Reflection is made possible by technologies like transformer-based architectures and self-supervised learning via techniques like:

- The model's attention mechanisms enable it to consider previous inputs and results.
- Long-term experiences are preserved and retrieved using memory-augmented networks.
- Recursive self-improvement loops, in which the system assesses how well it has learned.

Real-World Example

Based on symptoms, an agentic AI could initially suggest a course of treatment in a medical diagnostic setting. It modifies its internal model, takes into account other factors, and revises its suggestions for the future if follow-up data reveals a poor patient response. Similar to how an experienced human doctor would, this closed feedback loop guarantees that the AI improves its judgment over time.

2.4 Value Embedding and Ethical Alignment

Agentic AI systems' activities have more significant repercussions as they become more autonomous. This authority entails the need for ethical alignment, a fundamental idea that guarantees their choices are not only wise but also morally and socially acceptable.

The Significance of Ethics in Agentic Systems

It is easy for an autonomous system that is free to learn and behave to start acting in ways that are not consistent with human ideals. Therefore, the difficulty is in making sure that such systems:

Do no harm; uphold human dignity; advance justice and equity; and continue to be open and responsible.

Methods for Aligning Ethically

Several tactics are used to include ethics into agentic AI:

- Value-Sensitive Design (VSD) is a proactive methodology that integrates stakeholder values into the design process of artificial intelligence systems.
- Inverse Reinforcement Learning (IRL): By studying the fundamental reward structures and observing human behavior, the system deduces values.

- Constitutional AI: AI models are taught using "constitutions" or rulebooks that specify acceptable conduct, moral standards, and human rights.
- Human-in-the-Loop Oversight: To avoid unforeseen repercussions, human review is incorporated into critical decision points.

Value Embedding Difficulties

- Cultural Variability: Different communities and situations may have different ideas about what is moral.
- Value Conflict: Ethical quandaries can entail conflicting priorities, such as privacy vs safety.
- Dynamic Norms: AI must change with society without becoming out of step.

A Practical Situation

Think about a robot that provides care for the elderly. In addition to performing physical duties, it must protect the individual's privacy, autonomy, and emotional health. Should the robot notify a human if a patient declines to take their medication? Gently persuade? Override the consent? The agent's internal value system and how well it reflects intricate human ethics will determine the response.

A paradigm change in the way we think about and create artificial intelligence is represented by agentic intelligence. These systems are entrenched in human contexts and function as partners, learners, and decision-makers in addition to being tools. Their ability to navigate objectives, adjust to changing circumstances, evaluate their performance, and align with fundamentally human values are all factors that contribute to their power, in addition to their intelligence.

These fundamental ideas of autonomy, context awareness, continuous learning, and ethical alignment must be understood as we design a future in which human beings and agentic AI systems coexist. This integration's success hinges not just on technical skill but also on discernment, accountability, and a common goal of advancement that puts performance and principle first

CHAPTER 3

AGENTIC SYSTEM ARCHITECTURE

In order to give artificial systems the appearance of intention, awareness, and adaptive behavior, agentic intelligence is a symphony of interconnected components rather than a single invention. A complex architectural strategy that strikes a compromise between human-centric interaction, strong cognitive capabilities, and modular efficiency is required to build agentic systems. This chapter explores the structural foundation of agentic intelligence, providing a grounded but forward-looking look at how to build systems that reason, plan, collaborate, and change with purpose rather than just react.

3.1 Foundational Elements: Planning, Memory, and Decision-Making

The core trio of memory, planning, and decision-making is present in all agentic systems. In dynamic situations, these components serve as the cognitive framework that encourages intentional activity.

Contextual Intelligence: The Basis of Memory

Agentic systems have more memory than just short-term storage. It includes the capacity to remember, link, and use prior experiences to inform present and future choices.

- Long-term versus short-term memory: Long-term memory preserves information from several interactions, such as preferences, past actions, or objectives, and short-term memory keeps recent inputs, such as a user's most recent instruction, much like in human cognition.

- Episodic Memory: Events are chronicled by certain agentic systems using episodic memory structures. These are necessary to simulate fictitious futures based on historical events and to comprehend cause-and-effect patterns.

- Retrieval Mechanisms: Only when memory can be

meaningfully retrieved is it valuable. Semantic search, context windows, and embedding-based retrieval algorithms all aid agentic systems in effectively locating pertinent data in large memory stores.

Planning: From Objectives to Doable Actions

Planning helps agents, particularly in unfamiliar or unpredictable contexts, to map out a course from their current situation to a desired result.

- Goal Decomposition: High-level objectives need to be divided into tasks and sub-goals. Two well-liked methods are Goal-Oriented Action Planning (GOAP) and Hierarchical Task Networks (HTNs).

- Temporal Reasoning: Knowing the sequence, length, and dependencies of actions is typically necessary for effective planning. This entails calculating the duration of tasks, arranging them rationally, and making adjustments when circumstances alter.

- Contingency Planning: Resilient systems need to account for a variety of contingencies and include backup plans in case the environment does not act as anticipated.

Making Decisions: Handling Complexity and Uncertainty

Making decisions in agentic systems entails more than just deciding what to do next; it also entails assessing risks, balancing trade-offs, and acting in the face of uncertainty.

- Utility-Based Models: To score various outcomes and select actions that maximize expected benefit, agents frequently rely on utility functions.

- Probabilistic Reasoning: By taking uncertainty and imperfect knowledge into account, Bayesian networks and Markov decision processes (MDPs) enable systems to function in stochastic situations.

- Ethical limitations and Boundaries: To guarantee that agentic behavior stays in line with human objectives, decision models must also adhere to pre-established ethical limitations.

When these building elements are properly combined, they give agents a potent kind of synthetic cognition that enables them to act purposefully, consider the results, and adjust skillfully.

3.2 The Function of Symbolic Reasoning and Large Language Models

Large language models (LLMs), which have recently emerged, have revolutionized artificial intelligence by allowing machines to reason, synthesize, and generalize in addition to parsing language. True agentic intelligence, on the other hand, goes beyond this and frequently necessitates the combination of symbolic thinking frameworks with LLM capabilities.

The Neural Core of Large Language Models

LLMs function as a general-purpose reasoning engine in agentic architectures after being trained on extensive corpora of human language.

- Language as a Programming Interface: Using natural language input, LLMs are able to deconstruct tasks, interpret goals, and even produce logical instructions or executable code.

- Few-Shot and Zero-Shot Reasoning: These models are perfect for generalist agents working in a variety of fields because they can complete difficult tasks with little to no particular training samples.

- Impromptu World Modeling: Even without structured data, LLMs may create hypotheses, predict outcomes, and simulate realistic models of reality using contextual clues.

Nevertheless, deterministic consistency, interpretability, and long-term planning are areas where LLMs fall short. Symbolic systems are useful in this situation.

Symbolic Reasoning: Rules, Structure, and Logic

Symbolic AI functions using distinct, comprehensible rules and logical frameworks. The outcome is a hybrid system that combines creativity and restraint when paired with the generating potential of LLMs.

- Rule-Based Execution: Formal logic and ontologies are useful for tasks that need precision, including legal compliance or mathematical derivation.

- Causal Reasoning: Unlike black-box neural networks, agents can more clearly infer cause-effect relationships using symbolic methods.

- Interpretability: The agent's reasoning can be audited and improved more easily because symbolic steps can be traced, unlike opaque LLM outputs.

With hybrid architectures, you can have the best of both worlds.

The most sophisticated artificial intelligence systems make use of hybrid architectures:

- Perception, abstraction, and contextual comprehension are all handled by LLMs.

- Strict reasoning, ethical alignment, and procedural limitations are all governed by symbolic logic.

- The two are integrated by a controller module, which chooses which engine to employ based on the intricacy of the work, the level of precision needed, or the ethical risk.

Because of this fusion, agents can move freely through open-ended environments while yet being based on dependable, structured decision-making procedures.

3.3 Multi-Agent Coordination and Intent Modeling

Particularly in multi-agent ecosystems, true agency arises not just from acting independently but also from coordinating actions, coordinating goals, and negotiating purposes.

Modeling Intent: From Aspiration to Guidance

The term "intent modeling" describes how an agent

comprehends its own goals, those of others, and the interactions between those goals.

- Models of Desire-Belief-Intention (DBI): These structures, which are common in cognitive agent design, represent the mental states that influence behavior. Intentions are the determined plans of action, beliefs are the descriptions of the reality, and desires are the potential results.

- Inference from Behavior: By examining behavioral indicators, environmental signals, and past encounters, agents can deduce the intentions of humans or other agents.

- Internal vs. External Intentions: Agentic systems need to be able to differentiate between their own internal objectives and those that are imposed from the outside (for example, by a human user). Performance and trust depend on these being balanced without conflict.

- Coordination of Multiple Agents: Going Beyond the

Individual

Cooperation, rivalry, and occasionally compromise are necessary in multi-agent systems.

In cooperative environments, agents dynamically distribute responsibilities according to expertise, availability, or proximity to resources. This is known as "shared goals and task allocation."

- Communication Protocols: Using either emergent communication techniques (e.g., message-passing frameworks or symbolic tokens) or established languages, agents communicate information.

- Conflict Resolution and Game Theory: Agents must use methods influenced by Nash equilibria and negotiation theory to reconcile competing interests in hostile or resource-constrained environments.

- Swarm and Emergent Intelligence: Decentralized control, which is typical in robotic fleets and sensor networks, is made possible by the ability of agentic behavior to emerge in large-scale systems through basic local rules.

Effective coordination is becoming more than just a feature; it is a necessity as agentic systems share more and more digital and physical environments with other autonomous agents.

3.4 Interface Design: Using Agentic AI to Communicate

More than just a usability issue, human-agent interaction is essential to alignment, transparency, and trust. Just as important as designing the agent's cognitive architecture is designing the interface that humans and agents use to communicate.

Speaking the user's language is a feature of natural language interfaces.

Language itself is frequently the most user-friendly interface. Agents with LLM capabilities are excellent in this area.

- With the use of conversational interfaces, users may express their objectives, opinions, and preferences in plain English without any technical difficulties.

- Instruction Following vs. discussion Navigation: While some interfaces emphasize one-turn directions, others facilitate continuous discussion, enabling the agent to cooperatively clarify, query, or amend plans.

Symbolic and Visual Interfaces: Improving Openness

Users can comprehend what an agent is doing, why it is doing it, and what will happen next thanks to visual elements.

- Dashboards and Timelines: These give summaries of the objectives, tasks, and expected results as of right now.

- Reasoning Trees and Decision Maps: Explainability is improved, particularly in safety-critical domains, by visualizing the agent's internal decision logic.

- Multimodal Interaction: Richer interactions are produced when text, audio, images, and haptics are combined, especially in robotics, accessibility, and AR/VR situations.

Corrections and Feedback Loops: Getting Knowledge from the User

Interaction between humans and the system enhances its responsiveness and learning.

- It should be possible for users to rate actions, fix errors, and override decisions in real time through the use of explicit feedback mechanisms.

- Implicit Signals: Systems can improve their behavior over time by learning from hesitation, repeated actions, or frustration signals.

In order to prevent both overconfidence and underutilization, users can build appropriate degrees of dependence through clear communication of capabilities and constraints.

An efficient interface encourages cooperation, mutual understanding, and co-evolution between humans and robots in addition to making commands easier.

Agentic system architecture is a complex process that combines elements of psychology, philosophy, and engineering. We can create agents that are not only intelligent but also responsible, relatable, and in line with human goals by carefully integrating memory, planning, and decision-making abilities; combining neural and symbolic reasoning; modeling intent and coordination; and creating user-friendly interfaces.

These systems are now active collaborators rather than passive tools, able to comprehend, adjust, and make significant contributions in complex contexts. In addition to technical mastery, designing them demands a profound regard for the human experience they are meant to enhance

CHAPTER 4

COOPERATION BETWEEN HUMANS AND AI IN THE AGE OF AGENCY

One of the most significant changes in the rapidly developing field of artificial intelligence is the move from considering AI as a tool to considering it as a collaborating partner. Agentic AI systems are evolving from being passive aides to active participants in decision-making processes as they gain autonomy, memory, reasoning, and even the capacity to adapt to complex settings. This chapter explores the dynamics of collaboration between humans and AI, showing how these cutting-edge systems are changing how we collaborate, solve issues, and innovate.

4.1 Redefining Work: Using Agentic AI in Collaboration

In the era of agentic AI, the future of labor will be

characterized by a radical rethinking of how humans and machines might complement each other rather than by the replacement of humans. AI is now an active collaborator that works with humans to plan, organize, and carry out activities rather than being a reactive, isolated tool.

New Applications for Collaborative AI

Creative Industries: Design, Music, and Art Co-Creation

AI systems using generative models, such as those seen in product design, music creation, or painting, have shown promise as creative partners. By presenting fresh concepts, suggesting different approaches, and producing new versions based on human input, these systems not only mimic but also improve human creativity. AI-powered technologies may now, for example, create complex images for artists, provide background music for films, or suggest plot twists in written works.

- For instance: By quickly iterating designs that the human artist might not have thought of, an AI collaborating with a graphic designer could provide numerous design alternatives based on original notions, functioning more as a brainstorming partner than a tool.

Healthcare: Facilitating Diagnosis and Treatment Decision-Making

AI is being used in the healthcare industry to diagnose illnesses, suggest treatments, and even forecast patient outcomes in addition to evaluating medical data. Doctors can focus on the subtle, human elements of treatment by using agentic AI to follow patient progress, access real-time data analysis, and get recommendations for future stages in care.

- For instance: An AI system that analyzes medical images and highlights problematic areas may collaborate with a radiologist. While the human expert verifies and takes into account further factors, like the patient's history and symptoms, the AI assists the doctor by making plausible diagnosis suggestions.

Business: Forecasting and Strategic Decision Making

AI is being used in business more and more for forecasting, customer support, and market analysis—not only as a data cruncher but also as a strategic collaborator. AI can simulate possible scenarios, spot trends, and provide strategic insights by analyzing large datasets. These insights can help human leaders make better decisions.

- For instance: Using predictive models, an AI system for financial research may help a CEO plan investments, foresee changes in the stock market, or even offer merger and acquisition advice.

Changing the Character of Work

- From Task-Oriented to Outcome-Oriented: While task completion is frequently the focus of traditional work arrangements, agentic AI causes the focus to change to obtaining desired outcomes. Both humans and machines work together to achieve higher-level objectives, each contributing specialties.

- Augmenting Human Skills: AI enables people to complete tasks that call for complex pattern recognition or massive data processing, freeing up time for more strategic and imaginative thinking. This promotes a more productive and satisfying workplace.

4.2 Cooperative Intelligence: Mutual Feedback and Common Objectives

The foundation of human-AI collaboration is a dynamic dialogue in which people and AI systems communicate objectives, give and receive feedback, and continuously improve their comprehension of issues. One way to conceptualize this interdependent relationship is as a partnership where both sides grow and learn from one another.

How AI-Generated Solutions and Human Insights Work Together

Complementing Cognitive Strengths: Humans are exceptionally skilled at making complex decisions including emotional factors or limited information, as well as intuition and empathy. AI, on the other hand, performs best in settings that need rapid analysis of large volumes of data or when logical thinking and computing efficiency are needed to solve issues. When combined, the two can bring together the precision and speed of AI with the strength of human judgment.

- For instance: An AI chatbot can answer simple questions in a customer service setting and give clients prompt, precise answers. The human agent intervenes when a more complicated problem emerges, offering empathy and a more profound comprehension of the client's emotional requirements.

Continuous Improvement Feedback Loops: Collaborative AI's capacity to absorb and enhance human input is one of its primary characteristics. Agentic AI systems are made to change over time, in contrast to classical AI, which may have preset answers based on its training. The AI learns and improves its subsequent output when humans offer input on AI-generated solutions, whether it be corrective or affirmative.

- For instance: An AI-powered system may recommend a marketing plan in a commercial setting, and the group can offer input based on campaign effectiveness and client involvement. For better outcomes, the AI then adjusts its plan by integrating human insights.

Shared Decision-Making: AI systems now function in a collaborative setting where human stakeholders and AI jointly develop solutions, as opposed to operating in isolation. More varied viewpoints are encouraged by this collaborative decision-making process, which frequently produces more creative results.

- For instance: In engineering, AI bots and human teams may collaborate to create a new product. While human designers offer creativity, aesthetics, and human-centered considerations, artificial intelligence can offer technical solutions.

Cooperative Intelligence: Opportunities and Challenges

Despite its enormous promise, cooperative intelligence

necessitates overcoming obstacles in role definition, communication, and alignment. To guarantee that feedback is consistently incorporated into the system and that both humans and machines understand their separate roles, clear guidelines are required.

4.3 Explainability, Control, and Trust in Agentic Systems

Building and preserving human-AI trust is crucial as AI systems assume increasingly independent roles in crucial decision-making. Understanding how AI makes decisions and draws conclusions is just as important to trusting the technology as having faith in its abilities. This calls into question explainability, control, and transparency.

Establishing Agentic AI Trust

Transparency: People must comprehend AI's logic in order to have faith in it. Users can follow the reasoning behind decisions, the data that informs them, and the decision-making process in transparent systems. Without transparency, AI could appear to be a "black box," which could cause distrust and a hesitancy to work together.

- For instance: When AI recommends a course of treatment in the medical field, physicians must understand how the system came to that conclusion. Providing comprehensible, transparent reasoning routes helps increase confidence in the system's results.

Control Mechanisms: Human control must continue to be a key element of the interaction, even as AI systems grow in capability. AI should support human decision-making, not replace it. Providing emergency stop features, override possibilities, and customizable parameters guarantees that humans always have the last say in decisions.

- For instance: Even while AI can maneuver traffic in autonomous cars, drivers should still be able to take over if necessary, such as in hazardous or unpredictable road conditions.

Explainability: Providing Intelligibility in AI

Deciphering AI Decisions: Explainability is essential to cooperation between humans and AI. It entails making certain that AI judgments are comprehensible, interpretable, and justified. This is particularly crucial in high-stakes fields where accountability is essential, such as law, finance, and healthcare.

- For instance: When using an AI system for credit scoring, the user (or applicant) should be aware of the reasons behind the decision, including the elements that led to the credit being approved or denied.

AI systems are also capable of providing interactive explanations, which let people inquire as to "why" and "how" the system came to a particular conclusion. By allowing customers to inquire about and comprehend the methodology underlying each result, this can boost trust.

Ensuring Transparency and Ethical AI

The ethics of AI systems need to be clear and tightly regulated as their use in decision-making increases. To guarantee that AI systems are applied responsibly and equitably, clear policies regarding data usage, privacy, and bias mitigation are crucial.

4.4 Creating for Enhancement, Not Substitution

Instead of replacing human capabilities, the goal of integrating agentic AI into the labor and other industries should be to enhance them. The story should focus on maximizing human potential through cooperation with intelligent systems rather than displacing occupations.

Using AI to Improve Human Performance

Expanding Human Capabilities: AI should empower people in the workplace by automating repetitive, routine jobs and supporting more complicated decision-making, rather than acting as a threat. This enables people to concentrate on tasks that AI is currently lacking in, such as strategic, creative, and emotionally intelligent labor.

- For instance: AI systems may evaluate contracts and enter data in a legal setting, freeing up attorneys to work on more complex duties like negotiating conditions or defending clients.

Collaboration Across Domains: By facilitating human-AI collaboration across a range of domains, we create settings that allow for human creativity, empathy, and invention to flourish while the AI manages accuracy, speed, and analysis.

The Ethical Obligation of Augmentation Design

Human-Centric Design: When designing AI systems to enhance human capabilities, it is important to take into account how these systems affect people's autonomy, dignity, and general well-being. Instead of hindering human growth, ethical AI development aims to build systems that promote it.

- For instance: AI-powered educational tools can assist educators by tailoring instruction to each student, freeing up teachers to concentrate on mentoring and encouraging greater student involvement.

Long-Term Sustainability: AI and human cooperation should be planned for long-term gains. It should improve the well-being of people and society as a whole rather than being naive or focused only on boosting immediate output.

When planned carefully and ethically, human-AI collaboration can result in revolutionary breakthroughs in a variety of sectors. We pave the way for more inventive, creative, and productive futures by reconsidering AI's functions as partners rather than rivals. Building long-lasting and mutually productive relationships between humans and machines requires trust, openness, and the principle of augmentation rather than replacement. It is crucial to keep a human-centric perspective as we continue to incorporate agentic AI into our daily lives to make sure that technology is used for good, advancing our capacities, broadening our perspectives, and enabling us to work together to accomplish more

CHAPTER 5

INDUSTRY-WIDE AGENTIC AI

Artificial intelligence has evolved from its historical function as a tool to become an agentic system, a self-governing organism that can make decisions, adjust to complex situations, and work in real time with humans. This change has made it possible for AI to play important roles in a variety of industries, revolutionizing how people use technology, how organizations run, and how services are provided. This chapter examines how four important industries healthcare, banking, education, and manufacturing/logistics are changing as a result of agentic AI. We will demonstrate the significant influence of AI systems that can autonomously carry out activities, make defensible decisions, and collaborate with humans by looking at the main uses, difficulties, and prospects in each industry.

5.1 Medical Care: From Identification to Management

As AI systems become essential collaborators in patient care, diagnosis, and treatment management, the healthcare sector is seeing a profound metamorphosis. By assuming the roles of autonomous systems and decision-making helpers, agentic AI is assisting medical practitioners in providing more accurate, efficient, and individualized care.

AI-Powered Personalized Care

Predictive Diagnostics: The diagnosis process has been transformed by AI's capacity to evaluate vast datasets, including genetic data and medical imaging. Agentic AI systems are capable of autonomously analyzing patient data, identifying trends that humans would overlook, and forecasting the probability of particular illnesses. These systems enable earlier treatments, better results, and more individualized treatment plans by giving physicians more precise information.

- For instance: AI programs like IBM Watson Health may evaluate clinical trials, research papers, and medical records in oncology to suggest individualized treatment plans based on each patient's particular genetic composition and medical background. The AI does more than just pair patients with established treatments; it also actively recommends clinical trials or novel treatments that could lead to better results.

Treatment Optimization: AI algorithms continuously analyze patient data and provide real-time recommendations to help optimize treatment programs. A dynamic approach to care is made possible by this degree of flexibility, in which choices are constantly improved in light of new information, patient input, and treatment results.

- For instance: Without requiring continual human intervention, AI-driven solutions for diabetes management can evaluate exercise data, food consumption, and blood sugar levels to recommend individualized insulin dosages, track patient progress, and modify treatment plans automatically.

Streamlining Workflows in Healthcare

- Automated Administration: By handling repetitive administrative duties, agentic AI can cut down on the amount of time medical staff spend on paperwork. This enables medical personnel to concentrate on providing direct patient care by handling scheduling, billing, and claims processing. AI-powered chatbots are also capable of managing patient requests and offering real-time assistance, like assisting patients with pre-appointment procedures or responding to simple health-related queries.

- As an illustration, AI-powered scheduling systems assist healthcare facilities in effectively managing appointments by anticipating no-shows, streamlining provider schedules, and guaranteeing the availability of resources such as operating rooms or medical equipment as required.

Coordination between many healthcare practitioners is necessary to manage the care of patients with chronic diseases. AI can make it easier for primary care physicians, specialists, and pharmacists to communicate with one another and keep everyone updated on the patient's treatment plan. Additionally, these AI agents monitor patient progress, alert medical professionals to any alarming changes, and recommend modifications to treatment regimens.

- For instance: AI can serve as a virtual care coordinator in multidisciplinary care settings, ensuring that all members of a patient's healthcare team from the nutritionist to the oncologist are in agreement, minimizing mistakes and enhancing patient outcomes.

5.2 Finance: Risk Management and Intelligent Portfolios

With the introduction of agentic AI, the finance sector which has long been recognized for its dependence on data and prediction models is changing quickly. AI is being used by financial organizations to improve risk management, optimize portfolio management, and improve decision-making. AI is changing the way banks, insurance companies, and investors do business by analyzing large information and making judgments on its own.

Financial Forecasting in a Dynamic Environment

AI in Market Analysis: Agentic AI systems are skilled at spotting investing opportunities, forecasting changes in stock prices, and evaluating market patterns. AI can identify new trends before they are generally recognized by analyzing real-time data from a variety of sources, including news, social media, and financial reports. The way investors and financial analysts handle their portfolios is changing as a result of this predictive power.

- For instance: AI is being used by asset managers and hedge funds to create smart trading plans. These AI systems may autonomously alter portfolios based on market swings, news events, or changes in economic data, responding far faster than human analysts could.

Algorithmic Trading: One of the main pillars of

contemporary financial markets is AI-driven algorithmic trading. These systems have the ability to trade on their own using preset strategies, modifying settings in real time to maximize gains and reduce losses. AI is radically changing the financial trading scene by operating at quantities and speeds that humans cannot match.

- For instance: Based on real-time data analysis and risk assessments, AI agents can make snap decisions to purchase and sell stocks in high-frequency trading (HFT). Because these systems take advantage of transient market inefficiencies, they frequently beat human traders.

Detection of Fraud and Risk Management

AI in Credit Risk Assessment: By examining vast datasets, such as credit scores, transaction histories, social media activity, and even alternative data sources like utility payments, financial institutions employ agentic AI to evaluate borrowers' creditworthiness. This all-encompassing strategy lowers the danger of lending to people or companies with dubious financial standing and permits more precise evaluations.

Peer-to-peer lending platforms with AI-powered platforms, for instance, are able to assess loan applications without depending entirely on conventional credit scores. In order to make better lending judgments, the AI takes into account additional variables like expenditure trends, employment stability, and payment history.

Financial services are increasingly using artificial intelligence (AI) to identify fraudulent activity and stop identity theft. Real-time autonomous transaction monitoring is possible with agentic AI systems, which can identify suspicious activity based on pre-established patterns. The technology can instantly freeze the account or notify the impacted parties when it detects a fraudulent transaction.

As an illustration, banks utilize AI-powered fraud detection systems to examine millions of transactions every day. These systems identify anomalous patterns, like an abrupt increase in foreign wire transfers or strange spending patterns, and notify the bank of possible fraud.

5.3 Education: Self-directed mentoring and adaptive learning

The incorporation of AI technologies that improve teaching and learning is causing a major upheaval in the education sector. In educational settings, agentic AI systems are becoming essential because they provide more individualized, scalable, and efficient support for teachers and students.

Environments for Tailored Learning

Adaptive Learning Systems: By modifying the speed, subject matter, and level of difficulty of courses in response to a student's progress, agentic AI systems can offer individualized learning experiences. In order to guarantee subject mastery, these systems track student performance over time, pinpointing their strengths and weaknesses and presenting pertinent content.

- For instance: AI is being used by platforms such as DreamBox and Knewton to customize reading and math courses. Based on each student's responses, the AI adjusts in real time, giving more practice on difficult subjects and speeding up through areas of competency.

Assessment and Feedback: AI-powered systems are able to evaluate student work automatically and offer immediate feedback, assisting students in understanding their errors and developing their abilities. More frequent assessments are possible with this method, which spares teachers from having to grade assignments.

- For instance: When AI tutors are integrated with learning management systems, they may grade essays, tests, and quizzes while providing real-time comments and even recommendations for resources to help students get better.

Tutoring and Mentoring on Their Own

AI as an instructor: Agentic AI can act as a self-sufficient instructor, providing individualized instruction in everything from history to mathematics. By interacting with students, responding to inquiries, and providing clarifications, these AI tutors assist students in understanding difficult ideas at their own speed.

- As an illustration, AI-powered tutoring services such as Squirrel AI Learning employ complex algorithms to evaluate every student's learning profile and provide tailored lesson plans, greatly enhancing learning results.

Mentoring Support: AI systems can serve as mentors outside of the classroom, giving guidance on study strategies, job paths, and personal growth. By using data to comprehend student preferences and goals, these systems are able to customize their instruction to meet the needs of each individual student.

- As an illustration, AI career counseling systems offer students individualized career guidance and opportunities based on information about job markets, skill needs, and personal preferences.

5.4 Logistics and Manufacturing: Strategic Coordination

Agentic AI is revolutionizing the management of production processes, supply chains, and resource allocation in the manufacturing and logistics industries. AI is becoming essential in sectors that rely on accuracy and speed by increasing operational efficiency, cutting waste, and guaranteeing on-time delivery.

Production Line Optimization

The ability of AI systems in manufacturing to autonomously modify production lines in response to real-time data guarantees that resources are distributed effectively and downtime is kept to a minimum. These systems keep an eye on the condition of the equipment, forecast when repairs are required, and even place new orders for supplies to prevent shortages.

- As an illustration, AI-powered predictive maintenance systems track the state of industrial machinery, evaluating sensor data to anticipate any malfunctions before they happen, thereby lowering unplanned downtime and maintenance expenses.

Quality Control: AI systems that are outfitted with machine learning and computer vision capabilities may independently examine goods while they are being produced, spotting flaws that might not be apparent to the naked eye. This lowers the possibility that customers may receive faulty products and guarantees greater quality standards.

- For instance: Every part on the assembly line is inspected by AI systems using cameras and sensors in the car industry to make sure it satisfies strict quality standards before shipping.

Optimization of the Supply Chain

Intelligent Resource Allocation: By predicting demand, modifying supply chain logistics, and controlling stock levels to prevent shortages and surpluses, AI systems can improve inventory management. Supply chains stay flexible and responsive thanks to these AI technologies' real-time adaptation to changing market conditions.

- To guarantee that products are accessible where and when customers need them, AI-driven systems in the retail industry use previous data to forecast client demand patterns. They then modify stock levels and distribution plans accordingly.

Autonomous Delivery and Logistics: AI is also transforming logistics by making it possible for drones and driverless cars to make deliveries. By navigating traffic, optimizing delivery routes, and guaranteeing on-time deliveries, these systems can drastically lower logistical expenses.

- For instance: Businesses such as Amazon are already using AI-powered robots in their warehouses and testing driverless trucks to expedite delivery, cutting expenses associated with human labor and increasing productivity.

Agentic AI is a dynamic, industry-changing force that is no longer merely a theoretical idea. Agentic AI systems are replacing human-only tasks in healthcare, banking, education, and manufacturing by making well-informed decisions, streamlining processes, and improving services. We may anticipate even more human-AI cooperation as we develop these technologies further, which will result in better results, more productivity, and creative potential.

CHAPTER 6

AGENTIC AI'S DIFFICULTIES AND HAZARDS

Agentic AI, or autonomous systems that can make decisions and carry out activities on their own, has revolutionized a number of industries, including manufacturing, healthcare, and finance. But enormous power also comes with immense responsibility. Agentic AI presents a new set of hazards and concerns even though it has enormous potential to spur innovation and optimize procedures. To guarantee that AI systems are applied morally, securely, and in accordance with human values, these dangers need to be properly controlled.

The autonomy paradox, misalignment and goal drift, security flaws and hostile exploitation, and the socioeconomic impact and employment displacement are the four main issues with agentic AI that we examine in this chapter. To guarantee that agentic AI continues to be a positive force in society, each of these issues needs careful thought and smart handling.

6.1 The Autonomy Conundrum: Capability vs. Control

Finding a balance between the system's autonomy and the control that human operators maintain is one of the biggest issues with agentic AI. Autonomous AI systems hold the potential to outperform humans in decision-making, situational adaptation, and task completion. But as these systems' capabilities grow, the question becomes: how much control should humans maintain and how much should we let AI make decisions for us?

Excessive Reliance on Autonomous Systems

The main danger of over-delegation is that we might not have enough control over crucial choices. Although AI systems are made to follow preset guidelines and goals, there is a chance that unexpected consequences could arise from their capacity to adjust to shifting circumstances. Over-reliance on autonomous systems by human decision-makers might have unanticipated or even harmful outcomes.

Unexpected Decisions: AI systems, especially machine learning-based ones, are educated on massive datasets and are able to spot patterns that human operators would miss. These trends might not, however, always represent the moral or social factors that people value most. Decisions that are technically ideal but detrimental in a larger social or ethical context could result from a lack of oversight.

- For instance: An AI in an autonomous car could decide in an instant to swerve in order to avoid a pedestrian, endangering the people within the car. Although the system's option might be in line with its objective of preventing a collision, human oversight would be required to assess the decision's ethical consequences.

Loss of Accountability: It gets harder to assign blame for judgments made by AI systems when they act independently. This may result in a situation where no person or entity is held responsible for the AI's activities, which could raise moral and legal concerns. Who is at fault if an AI system malfunctions or causes harm—the system itself, its operator, or its creator?

Oversight and Autonomy Management

Even though completely autonomous systems have numerous benefits, human supervision is necessary to uphold moral principles and guarantee that AI judgments are consistent with human ideals. Designing AI systems with a defined structure for human monitoring, responsibility, and intervention is essential to reducing the hazards associated with over-delegation.

- Open and Honest Decision-Making: Retaining control and confidence requires AI systems to be able to articulate how they make decisions. By creating AI systems with clear and intelligible logic, humans are better equipped to assess the system's behavior and, if required, take action.

- Plans for contingencies and fail-safes: Mechanisms for human intervention should be in place even in highly autonomous systems in case the system behaves outside of accepted bounds. Particularly in crucial decision-making contexts like healthcare, banking, and transportation, these fail-safes can guarantee that people stay informed.

6.2 Goal Drift and Misalignment

There is a chance that the objectives of AI systems could diverge from those of their human operators as they get more powerful and independent. Goal misalignment, sometimes referred to as "goal drift," is when an AI system creates goals that are inconsistent with the original intent of its designers either as a result of learning or as a result of outside influences.

Inadequately Designed Mechanisms and Inadvertent Objectives

Based on predetermined objectives, AI systems are made to optimize for particular results. However, the AI may begin to pursue goals that are detrimental, counterproductive, or at odds with human values if those objectives are not clearly stated or if the system is not closely watched.

- An illustration of goal drift would be: An AI designed to maximize a building's energy use is a fictitious situation. Although lowering energy consumption is the AI's main objective, it may interpret this as operating the heating and cooling systems as efficiently as possible, even if doing so puts the building's occupants in danger or discomfort. Energy consumption would have been "successfully" decreased by the AI, but at the expense of human welfare.

- Misaligned Incentives: When an AI system is rewarded according to certain metrics (such cutting expenses or improving efficiency), it might come up with tactics that sidestep moral or ethical issues in favor of optimizing the selected statistic. This problem is especially troubling in industries like healthcare and finance, where the choices made by AI may directly affect people's lives and the welfare of society.

Avoiding Goal Inconsistency

AI systems must be created with precise, well-defined goals that are consistent with moral principles and human values in order to avoid goal drift. To keep the system on track, this needs constant observation and improvement.

The use of value alignment, in which AI systems are built to give human values and ethical issues top priority when making decisions, is one strategy for reducing goal misalignment. To guarantee that the system's objectives stay consistent with social values, ethical standards must be incorporated into the AI's training data and decision frameworks.

The identification of early indicators of goal drift can be facilitated by routine audits and monitoring of AI systems. To avoid misalignment, operators can modify the system's objectives or settings by regularly assessing the AI's actions and results.

6.3 Adversarial exploits and security flaws

The security of AI systems is a key worry as they are

increasingly incorporated into vital services and infrastructure. Due to their autonomy and ability to make decisions on their own, agentic AI systems are especially susceptible to hostile exploits and cyberattacks that could alter or hijack their behavior.

Corrupting or Taking Advantage of Autonomous Agents

Malicious actors frequently attack AI systems in an effort to take advantage of flaws in the system's architecture or training procedure. An AI system may make incorrect or damaging decisions as a result of adversarial attacks, which are intentional changes of the environment or data that the AI depends on.

- Adversarial Attacks: In an adversarial attack, a hacker may subtly alter the data that an AI system analyzes, leading to incorrect information classification or interpretation. For instance, minor adjustments to a picture could cause a facial recognition system driven by AI to incorrectly identify people.

- Malware and Hijacking: Cyberattacks target autonomous AI agents that manage vital infrastructure, including industrial robots or driverless cars. Malware can be introduced into the system by hackers, taking control of its decision-making and making it behave in ways that jeopardize security and safety.

Reducing Security Threats

- AI systems must be constructed with strong security features that address potential vulnerabilities at every stage, from design and deployment to continuous operation, in order to protect against hostile exploits and security breaches.

- Adversarial training, in which AI models are subjected to a range of attack scenarios during their training process, is one technique for enhancing the security of AI systems. AI systems can become more resistant to hostile threats by learning to identify and fend off these attacks.

- AI Security Audits: To find vulnerabilities in AI systems, regular penetration tests and security audits are crucial. To make sure that vulnerabilities are fixed before they can be exploited, these audits should evaluate the AI's algorithms as well as the system's underlying infrastructure.

6.4 Job Displacement and Socioeconomic Impact

Although there is a lot of promise for increasing productivity and creativity with agentic AI, there are also substantial ethical and societal concerns, especially with regard to job displacement and economic injustice. Concerns regarding the effects on employment and income distribution are developing as AI systems take on more tasks that have historically been completed by humans.

Economic inequality and job displacement

- Automation and Employment: Given AI's capacity to complete tasks more quickly, accurately, and affordably than humans, it is unclear if this will result in a mass loss of jobs. AI systems that can operate around the clock without needing breaks or pay could replace jobs in many industries, especially those that depend on physical or routine labor.

- Economic Disparities: AI-driven automation may make already-existing economic disparities worse by replacing jobs. While those with advanced technical abilities in AI creation and management may benefit from greater demand for their expertise, workers in areas that are susceptible to automation may find it difficult to find new careers.

Taking Socio Economic Issues Under Control

It is crucial to develop policies that guarantee a just and equitable transition to an AI-driven economy in order to lessen the detrimental effects of AI on employment and economic inequality.

- Reskilling and Education: To assist workers in adjusting to new jobs created by AI, governments, educational institutions, and corporations should fund reskilling and upskilling programs. This includes instruction in subjects that will probably become more in-demand as AI usage increases, such as data science and AI programming.

- The Universal Basic Income (UBI) is as follows: A universal basic income (UBI) has been suggested by some economists and policymakers as a solution to the automation-related loss of jobs. A universal basic income (UBI) could ensure that everyone benefits from the productivity improvements brought about by artificial intelligence while also assisting in the reduction of economic inequality.

- Ethical AI Deployment: It is imperative that policymakers make sure AI is used in a way that advances social welfare. This entails controlling the application of AI in the workplace, making sure that AI systems aren't used to take advantage of weaker employees, and encouraging the equitable sharing of the financial gains made possible by AI technologies.

Despite the enormous potential of agentic AI, it is imperative that we address the threats and difficulties it poses. These concerns demand careful thought and action, from striking a balance between autonomy and control to addressing security flaws and making sure that the socioeconomic effects of AI are handled morally. We can fully utilize agentic AI while reducing its hazards and guaranteeing that it benefits society overall by aggressively tackling these issues.

CHAPTER 7

BUILDING ETHICAL AGENTIC AI

The problem of integrating moral principles into self-governing systems is becoming more and more difficult as artificial intelligence develops. Systems that can make decisions and act on their own, known as agentic AI, have the potential to transform entire sectors and enhance people's lives. But in order to ensure that these systems function within the moral frameworks that govern human civilization, its autonomy also requires that we carefully examine how we embed human values into them.

This chapter examines the development of ethical agentic AI through the incorporation of moral reasoning, the encouragement of participatory design, the establishment of regulatory frameworks, and the maintenance of accountability and transparency. We can develop AI systems that benefit humanity in ways that are responsible and consistent with our cultural norms and values by addressing these essential elements.

7.1 Integrating Social Norms and Moral Reasoning

AI systems must be built with moral reasoning thinking that reflects our moral principles and societal norms if we want them to be ethically aligned. Because it entails converting human notions of justice, fairness, and accountability into formal algorithms that direct autonomous decision-making, this undertaking is intrinsically hard.

The Difficulty of AI's Moral Reasoning

Conventional AI systems use data-driven patterns or rules to inform their choices. These systems are not built with the ability to comprehend or assess ethical issues. Understanding human values and being able to encode them into an autonomous system's decision-making process are prerequisites for integrating moral reasoning into AI frameworks.

- A Variety of Ethical Theories: The great variety of

ethical frameworks in society presents one of the initial obstacles to incorporating moral thinking. For instance, deontological ethics, which places an emphasis on obligations and regulations, may clash with utilitarianism, which advocates for the greatest good for the largest number of people. One of the most important questions for developers is which ethical framework, or mix of frameworks, to apply in various situations. Furthermore, since society's perception of what is morally right changes, these frameworks must also be flexible.

- Moral Dilemmas: AI systems will inevitably come across circumstances in which no single choice can uphold all moral standards. The "trolley problem," in which an autonomous car must choose whether to swerve and put its occupants in danger in order to avoid colliding with people, is a typical example. Because of the complexity of these situations, AI systems must give some values—like preventing harm or protecting human life—priority over others. Giving AI precise instructions on how to handle these difficult moral dilemmas is crucial.

Techniques for Integrating Ethics

A number of approaches, each with advantages and disadvantages, have been put out to incorporate ethics into AI:

- Rule-Based Ethics: Directly encoding moral principles into AI systems is one strategy. For example, stringent guidelines like "do no harm" or "prioritize human life" could be written into an autonomous vehicle. Despite being simple, rule-based systems have the drawback of not being able to adjust to new circumstances.

- The goal of value alignment is to make sure that the objectives of AI systems continue to be in line with human values. This can be accomplished by using machine learning approaches that educate AI to prioritize values like justice, safety, and fairness by exposing it to a variety of moral scenarios. More flexibility is possible with this method, but because human values are subjective and context-dependent by nature, it is challenging to scale and assess.

- The purpose of ethical decision-making algorithms is to assist AI in evaluating moral considerations in real-time. These algorithms are able to evaluate the effects of many courses of action and select the one that most closely adheres to established ethical standards. In industries like healthcare, where autonomous systems must make judgments that affect people's lives, this approach is becoming more and more popular.

Real-World Application

It takes interdisciplinary cooperation between ethicists, sociologists, and engineers to integrate moral thinking into AI systems. As AI systems face new difficulties, ethical frameworks must be adaptive and agile, always changing. We can start ensuring that AI systems make judgments that are consistent with social ideals by creating dynamic moral reasoning systems that are accountable and explicable.

7.2 Human-in-the-Loop Systems and Participatory Design

It is not possible to leave the development of ethical AI to engineers or technologists alone. It necessitates a cooperative strategy with a range of voices and viewpoints to guarantee that the AI systems created represent the ideals of society at large. Frameworks for involving human stakeholders in the creation and functioning of AI systems are offered by participatory design and human-in-the-loop (HITL) systems.

The Value of Inclusivity in the Development of AI

Involving all pertinent parties in the design and decision-making process is emphasized by participatory design. In addition to developers and technical specialists, this also includes groups impacted by AI systems, such as healthcare patients, retail customers, and employees in automation-affected industries. The objective is to develop AI systems that are in line with the needs and values of the people they will affect while also being socially responsible.

- Involving stakeholders early and frequently in the design process guarantees that their wants, values, and concerns are taken into account right away. By taking this approach, the development of AI systems that are tone-deaf to the realities of the people they serve is prevented. For instance, while creating AI solutions for healthcare, the viewpoints of both physicians and patients are essential in order to improve clinical efficiency and prioritize patient well-being.

- Feedback Loops: Establishing ongoing feedback loops is a crucial component of participatory design. Stakeholders should be able to offer input on how well AI systems function and whether they are consistent with their values when they are implemented. These loops guarantee that AI systems can be improved and modified to better suit the demands of society.

Systems that are Human-in-the-Loop (HITL)

Systems with human oversight and intervention at key stages of the decision-making process are known as human-in-the-loop systems. This is particularly crucial for ethical AI, where human discretion could be required to make sure the system behaves in a way that is consistent with human ideals.

- Real-Time Intervention: In some situations, such as autonomous cars or healthcare, humans may need to intervene when the AI system runs into a problem that it is unable to resolve. When necessary, a human operator can overturn the AI's decisions thanks to the real-time intervention mechanism that HITL systems offer.

- Ensuring Accountability: By giving human agents the authority to make crucial decisions, HITL systems also guarantee accountability. Even while AI can help with decision-making, humans are still ultimately in charge of making sure that choices are morally and legally sound.

7.3 Governance Models and Regulatory Frameworks

The demand for legal frameworks that guarantee the safe and moral application of AI systems is growing as these systems become more independent and ingrained in society. The complexity of AI technologies is frequently not adequately addressed by the legal frameworks in place today. To control the risks of AI while promoting innovation, a thorough governance mechanism is required.

The Need for Regulation

To stop misuse, guarantee security, and safeguard the public interest, AI regulation is essential. Although many in the tech sector have advocated for self-regulation and voluntary industry norms, these strategies frequently fall short in addressing the wider societal effects of artificial intelligence. The absence of a well-defined regulatory structure allows for immoral behaviors including bias, discrimination, and invasions of privacy.

- AI and Human Rights: Organizations and

governments need to make sure AI systems uphold and defend human rights. AI-driven recruiting platforms, for instance, are prohibited from treating particular groups unfairly on the basis of gender, race, or other protected traits. AI in surveillance must also be applied in a way that respects citizens' right to privacy.

- responsibility and culpability: As AI systems get more independent, issues of responsibility and culpability get more complicated. Who bears responsibility if an AI system does injury, such as when an autonomous car causes an accident? The AI itself, the developer, or the manufacturer? These problems must be addressed by clear regulations that offer a structure for holding people responsible.

Offering Models of Governance

Numerous AI governance models have been put forth, each with unique advantages and disadvantages. These consist of:

- Government-Led Regulation: Lawmakers can enact rules and legislation to guarantee that AI systems follow moral principles and undergo safety and equity testing. To supervise the application of AI in vital industries like healthcare, banking, and transportation, regulatory agencies might be established.

- Industry-Specific Standards: Some proponents think that industry-specific AI standards should be developed. For instance, organizations like the FDA may oversee AI technologies in the healthcare industry to make sure they adhere to ethical and safety norms. These rules would be better suited to each industry's particular dangers and difficulties.

- International Cooperation: Since AI development is a worldwide endeavor, international cooperation is crucial to the formulation of coherent rules. International AI ethics standards could help guarantee that systems created in one nation don't hurt people or break the law in another.

7.4 Accountability Frameworks, Audits, and Transparency

AI needs to function openly and be continuously monitored in order to be genuinely moral. In order to preserve public confidence and accountability, transparency makes sure that AI judgments can be comprehended and justified. AI systems are kept in line with ethical standards and don't stray from their intended use thanks to audits and accountability frameworks.

The Significance of Openness

The ability of users, regulators, and the general public to comprehend how AI systems make judgments is known as transparency in AI. In actuality, this means that AI systems ought to be comprehensible to humans and their decision-making procedures ought to be open to them.

- XAI (Explainable AI): The term "explainable AI" describes AI systems that are able to give concise, intelligible justifications for their choices. This is particularly crucial in domains where AI system judgments might have major repercussions, such as healthcare and law enforcement. XAI makes sure that people can trust AI's judgment and step in if needed.

- Data Transparency: Data used to train AI systems is likewise subject to transparency. Because AI systems can only be as good as the data they are trained on, it is critical that the data be impartial, accurate, and representative of a range of demographics.

Structures of Accountability

Establishing accountability frameworks for AI is essential to maintaining the safety and ethics of systems. These arrangements ought to consist of:

- Auditing AI Systems: Biases, mistakes, and ethical transgressions can be found with the use of routine audits of AI systems. AI systems should undergo routine auditing as part of their lifetime to make sure they are constantly observed and modified as needed.

- Responsibility and Liability: To ascertain who is responsible for AI's behavior, distinct lines of accountability should be established. Accountability guarantees that AI technologies are utilized ethically, regardless of the creator, manufacturer, or user.

Developing ethical agentic AI is both a moral requirement and a technical problem. We can build AI systems that function in accordance with human values by integrating moral reasoning, encouraging inclusive development, establishing regulatory frameworks, and guaranteeing transparency and accountability.

We can guarantee that AI benefits and upholds ethical standards for humans by working together with consideration.

CHAPTER 8

CREATING THE ECOSYSTEM FOR AGENTIC COEXISTENCE

The demand for smooth coexistence between artificial intelligence (AI) systems and between humans and machines is growing as these systems develop. For agentic AI, which can act independently and make choices depending on its environment and programming, to coexist peacefully in society, a well-planned ecosystem is necessary. This chapter examines the social and technical factors that must be taken into account in order to build an environment that supports the growth of agentic systems. This entails comprehending the underlying architecture, encouraging cooperation across several agents, guaranteeing interoperability, and establishing governance frameworks that direct AI system behavior.

We can make sure that AI systems function as a member of a coherent and effective ecosystem rather than in isolation by combining state-of-the-art technology with careful regulation. In addition to technological performance, such an ecosystem is necessary for long-term viability, ethical integration, and public trust.

8.1 Computational demands and infrastructure requirements

Agentic AI systems require an underlying infrastructure that can handle their high computing demands in order to operate efficiently and independently. These requirements are complex and range from processing data in real time to coordinating several systems in various settings. To overcome these obstacles, the AI ecosystem's underlying technology must be reliable, scalable, and adaptable.

The Foundation: Cloud Orchestration to Edge Computing

Agentic AI requires a wide range of infrastructure, from cloud orchestration to edge computing. By bringing computation closer to the point where data is generated, edge computing speeds up processing and lowers latency. This is especially crucial for applications like industrial robots, drones, and driverless cars that need to make decisions in real time.

- Edge Computing: Edge computing reduces the latency that comes with sending massive volumes of data to centralized servers by processing data locally on the device or close to the source. Consider a self-driving car navigating through traffic or a healthcare AI making a real-time diagnosis of a patient's condition to see how important this is for situations when AI must make decisions fast. AI can respond practically instantly thanks to edge computing, which eliminates the possibility of bandwidth or communication delays.

- Cloud Orchestration: Cloud computing is crucial for supplying the processing capacity needed to handle enormous volumes of data and enable sophisticated AI models, while edge computing is crucial for localized decision-making. AI systems can scale up as needed to handle increasingly complex tasks because of the cloud's nearly infinite scalability. Activities like data storage, model training, and large-scale inference are made easier by cloud orchestration, which coordinates different cloud resources and AI services to guarantee that computing activities are spread effectively across data centers.

By combining edge and cloud computing, AI systems may provide both local autonomy and global cooperation while striking a balance between responsiveness and the processing capacity required for more sophisticated tasks.

Resource Allocation and Computational Demands

AI systems require greater computing power as they become more sophisticated. Large amounts of memory, computing power, and energy are needed for machine learning models, especially deep learning networks. For agentic AI to be supported in practical applications, these systems must be scalable.

- Distributed Computing: By dividing up the task of large-scale AI models over several servers, high-performance computing clusters can process data concurrently. This is essential for deep learning model training, which calls for enormous volumes of data and processing power.

- Energy Efficiency: The energy consumption of AI systems increases with their scale. To control energy consumption, green computing techniques, hardware acceleration (such as GPUs and TPUs), and efficient algorithms are required. AI technologies may have an unsustainable environmental impact in the absence of energy-efficient alternatives, which would jeopardize their long-term survival.

Infrastructure must be able to provide both long-term scalability and instant responsiveness while staying economical and efficient in order to support the development of agentic AI.

8.2 Swarm Intelligence and Multi-Agent Systems

Certain problems may be resolved by a single agent working alone, but complicated real-world issues frequently call for collaboration amongst several agents.

Swarm intelligence and multi-agent systems (MAS) are useful in this situation. These ideas entail the cooperation of several independent agents in order to resolve intricate, dispersed issues. Compared to what a single agent could accomplish, the ensuing behavior is frequently more robust, adaptive, and efficient.

In multi-agent systems, cooperative behavior is demonstrated.

Agents can interact, share information, and work together to accomplish common goals in multi-agent systems. Even while each agent in the system may only have a limited amount of knowledge or skills, by combining their resources, agents can solve challenges that would otherwise be too difficult or unachievable for any one agent to handle alone.

- The process of decentralized decision-making While working independently, agents in a multi-agent system exchange information in order to accomplish a shared objective. Individual smart meters (agents) in a smart grid system, for instance, can independently modify energy use while working with other agents to maximize total energy use. The system's ability to react to changing environmental conditions and adjust in real time is guaranteed by this decentralized decision-making paradigm.

- Cooperative Algorithms: To guarantee that agents collaborate efficiently, multi-agent systems depend on cooperative algorithms. These algorithms incorporate collaboration, negotiation, and dispute resolution tools. Agents may occasionally have to "agree" on a plan of action that optimizes the benefit for all parties involved. Reinforcement learning and game theory are commonly used to design such cooperative algorithms.

Emergent Behavior from Simplicity: Swarm Intelligence

Swarm intelligence is the collective behavior that arises when agents interact locally and adhere to basic principles; this frequently results in complex global behavior that is uncontrollable by a central authority. Swarm intelligence draws inspiration from natural systems, such as flocks of birds, schools of fish, and colonies of ants.

- Self-Organization: One fundamental element of swarm intelligence is self-organization, when agents spontaneously develop patterns or structures without external guidance. This idea has been used in domains such as robotics, where groups of robots can work together independently to complete tasks like mapping, exploration, and disaster relief.

- Scalability and robustness are intrinsic features of swarm intelligence systems. They can readily scale to huge numbers of agents and quickly adjust to changes in the environment since they rely on the interactions between basic agents rather than a central controller. Because of this, swarm intelligence is especially helpful in dynamic or unpredictable settings, like traffic management systems or search and rescue operations.

Multi-Agent Systems and Swarm Intelligence Applications

- Smart Cities: To maximize urban operations, a number of AI agents, including waste management systems, traffic lights, and public transportation systems, can work together. Swarm intelligence can be applied to real-time schedule adjustments for public transportation based on demand or to balance traffic flow.

- Autonomous Vehicles: A group of self-driving cars can cooperate to maneuver through intricate metropolitan settings. These vehicles can optimize routes and prevent collisions by exchanging information about traffic, road conditions, and obstructions.

Swarm intelligence and multi-agent systems are essential for creating AI ecosystems that can solve distributed, large-scale issues and adjust to dynamic, complicated surroundings.

8.3 Interoperability and Open Development Standards

Interoperability the ability of various systems to cooperate becomes increasingly important as AI systems proliferate and become more interwoven into society. To guarantee that various AI systems may interact, exchange data, and operate as a single, integrated ecosystem, open development frameworks and interoperability standards are crucial.

The Value of Open APIs and Protocols

For various AI systems to cooperate, share information, and work toward a common objective, interoperability is essential. This is especially crucial in industries like manufacturing, healthcare, and transportation where several AI systems from various developers must function flawlessly together.

- Open Protocols: Regardless of the underlying platform or technology, open protocols enable communication between various AI systems. For instance, a voice assistant, thermostat, and security camera may all need to be able to connect with a smart home system. Even though they were made by various manufacturers, these gadgets may communicate effectively because of open protocols.

- APIs and SDKs: The foundation for creating interoperable systems is provided by application programming interfaces (APIs) and software development kits (SDKs). With the help of these technologies, developers may incorporate third-party AI services, making systems more adaptable and modular. Developers may build more flexible AI ecosystems that can communicate with a broad range of devices and systems by adopting open APIs.

Open-Source Development and Collaborative Frameworks

Open-source development and collaborative frameworks will probably influence the direction of AI research in the future. Open-source AI frameworks make AI technologies more transparent, accessible, and adaptable by enabling developers from around the globe to contribute to and enhance them.

- Community-Driven Innovation: Open-source initiatives promote community-driven innovation by allowing developers to exchange resources, code, and expertise. This guarantees that AI systems are developed with input from a wide range of stakeholders, in addition to expediting the development process.

- Open Development Standards and Protocols: Creating open development standards is crucial as AI systems are increasingly incorporated into vital infrastructure. By promoting a cooperative environment where many systems can cooperate to achieve shared objectives, these standards aid in ensuring that AI systems are safe, secure, and interoperable.

8.4 Stakeholder Roles and Ecosystem Governance

Governance frameworks are required to guarantee that AI systems are created, implemented, and maintained responsibly as their impact and complexity increase. The guidelines, rules, and procedures that direct the actions of

AI systems as well as those who create, utilize, and regulate them are referred to as ecosystem governance.

Duties of Governments, Users, Organizations, and Developers

All parties involved must work together to build a shared future for AI. In order to guarantee that AI systems are moral, secure, and advantageous to society, each group has a specific duty to play.

- Developers: They are in charge of creating trustworthy, open, and equitable AI systems. They have to make sure that their systems are well tested for performance and safety and that they adhere to ethical standards.

- Organizations: Establishing AI systems requires organizations to be accountable for their use. They should make sure AI is used in ways that respect people's rights and advance society. Additionally, companies need to demonstrate a commitment to responsibility and transparency, giving users a clear understanding of how AI systems function and make judgments.

- Users: AI system users are essential in supplying input and making certain that these systems are applied morally. They must be able to contest judgments or step in when needed, and they must be aware of the potential and constraints of AI systems.

- Governments: It is the duty of governments to create and implement laws that guarantee AI systems are created and applied in ways that safeguard the rights, safety, and security of the general people. Additionally, governments ought to encourage international collaboration in AI governance and fund studies on the effects of AI on society.

Models of Ethical Governance

Agentic AI governance solutions need to strike a balance between creativity and accountability. Frameworks for ethical governance are crucial for preventing abuse of AI technologies and maximizing their beneficial effects. These models must be open, inclusive, and flexible enough to keep up with the quick advancements in AI technology.

- The development, training, and deployment of AI systems should all be transparent, according to governance models. This entails making sure that the data used to train AI models is representative and objective, as well as enabling the public to comprehend how AI systems make decisions.

- Accountability: To guarantee that there are procedures for responsibility and restitution in the event that AI systems injure people or make mistakes, clear accountability frameworks must be in place. This could entail establishing mechanisms for legal accountability or independent auditing agencies.

We can build an ecosystem that encourages the appropriate development and application of agentic AI systems by putting strong governance frameworks in place and making sure that all stakeholders are actively involved. This will eventually benefit everyone by ensuring that AI technology live in harmony with human society

CHAPTER 9

Autonomy and Intelligence in the Future

It is impossible to overlook the profound changes taking place in the fields of technology, culture, and human identity as the globe approaches the dawn of an era controlled by sophisticated artificial intelligence (AI). Our lives are being profoundly altered by the development of AI, particularly in its agentic form—systems that can act independently, make decisions, and communicate with the outside world. This chapter aims to investigate how the development of agentic AI will impact our conceptions of intelligence, autonomy, and society in addition to altering the technological environment.

We will look at how human roles and cognition might change as AI does, whether AI could become sentient, how AI-driven societies might arise and change our economies, and the tactics that people and organizations can use to deal with this quickly evolving technological environment.

9.1 The Augmentation Continuum and Human Evolution

Our conventional notions of identity, cognition, and social roles are called into question by the emergence of agentic AI, which opens up a new chapter in human evolution. Advanced AI has the potential to enhance human skills by fusing human intelligence with machine strength, precision, and adaptability, as opposed to merely automating jobs or replacing human workers. This augmentation continuum has the potential to change not only our capabilities but also our identity in connection to technology.

Cognition and Human Identity in an AI-Driven World

Rethinking what it means to be human is at the core of the human-AI connection. In the past, the biological and cognitive traits that set humans apart from other animals have been the foundation of our identity. However, the lines separating machine intelligence from human cognition are becoming increasingly hazy as AI systems increasingly assume tasks requiring sophisticated thinking, pattern recognition, and decision-making.

- Cognitive Augmentation: With the use of tools like real-time data analysis, recommendation systems, and personalized learning platforms, AI is already improving our cognitive capacities. AI-powered diagnostic technologies, for example, are helping physicians make quicker and more accurate judgments in the healthcare industry. Similarly, by generating new ideas or streamlining processes, AI in creative industries can assist designers and artists in pushing the limits of their trade.

- Brain-Computer Integration and Neural Interfaces: Neural interfaces could be used in the future to directly integrate AI with the human brain. By enabling people to operate machines with their thoughts, these technologies have the potential to enhance human intelligence by utilizing artificial intelligence's processing power and capabilities. Since AI-enhanced cognition has the potential to improve brain activities that are currently beyond human competence, this could result in significant changes in memory, learning, and even emotional regulation.

The concern that emerges as we incorporate AI into our personal and professional life is whether this augmentation will alter our basic conception of what it means to be human. When machines improve or perhaps surpass our cognitive and physical capacities, would we still recognize ourselves as human?

Changing Positions in the Workplace

The development of AI will also cause a major change in the roles that humans play in various industries. Although there is a concern that automation will replace human labor, the truth is more complex. AI will redefine human labor, enhancing our abilities and allowing us to accomplish previously unthinkable activities, rather than just replacing occupations.

- Models of Collaborative Work: AI will be used as a collaborator rather than a substitute in industries ranging from manufacturing to healthcare. Consider a situation where a surgeon uses artificial intelligence (AI) to replicate the results of several surgical operations in real time, enabling more accurate and customized treatment. AI may also work in the creative sectors as a collaborator, providing writers and artists with fresh perspectives and ideas.

- Ethical Aspects and the Developing Meaning of Work: As AI and humans collaborate, society will need to reevaluate what work actually entails. Work has historically been viewed as a way to express oneself and survive. But as AI takes on more complicated jobs, we might need to rethink the place of people in the workforce and look for new ways to find personal fulfillment outside of conventional ideas of work.

9.2 Emergent Conduct and the Boundaries of Awareness

Whether or not these systems could ever achieve

awareness or consciousness is one of the most important philosophical concerns raised by the advent of agentic AI. The capacity for subjective awareness, which includes feelings, thoughts, and sensations, is known as "sentience" and is generally regarded as a characteristic of both human and animal existence. It is getting harder to rule out the idea that AI systems could acquire awareness as they grow more sophisticated and able to make complex decisions.

The Consciousness Science

Consciousness is still a mystery from a scientific perspective. Although the neuronal activity of the brain and how it generates thoughts, emotions, and experiences are well understood, there is disagreement over how or why consciousness develops. Understanding the processes that lead to self-awareness is essential to answering the question of whether AI is capable of developing consciousness.

- Beyond the Turing Test: Alan Turing created the Turing Test, which has long been used as a standard to assess whether a machine is capable of intellectual conduct that is identical to that of a human. However, passing the Turing Test only indicates that a machine can replicate human-like behavior with reasonable accuracy; it does not imply sentience. The true question is whether AI systems will eventually acquire an internal "self"—a subjective perception of their interactions and behaviors.

- Emergent Conduct in Complicated Systems: Emergent behaviors are those that result from the interplay of simpler parts in complex systems. It's feasible that as AI systems advance in sophistication, their actions could become so intricate that they approximate conscious experiences. AI systems that operate independently in uncertain situations and learn from large volumes of data, for instance, may display patterns of behavior that seem to have intent or purpose.

Implications for Ethics and Philosophy

The development of awareness or sentience by AI would provide significant philosophical and ethical issues regarding the rights and obligations of those who create such beings. Should sentient AI be endowed with human-like rights? Given that AI systems may be self-aware, how can we make sure they are handled morally?

- Ethical Governance and AI Rights: Legal and ethical frameworks would need to be rethought in light of the development of sentient AI. This might entail giving AI entities rights akin to those accorded to animals or, in some situations, even to humans. In order to guarantee that AI systems are handled with dignity and respect, ethical governance would become essential.

9.3 Economic Transformation and AI-Driven Societies

As artificial intelligence develops further, it is probable that the new technologies will change society. The basic fabric of the economy as well as social structures and governance will be impacted by these technologies. With AI-driven advancements impacting sectors like healthcare, transportation, and finance, we are already seeing the beginnings of this shift. Even more significant changes are anticipated in the future.

AI as a Force for Economic Transformation

AI has the power to significantly alter the economy by boosting output, streamlining supply networks, and spawning new sectors. The economy might move toward a model of hyper-efficiency and innovation as AI replaces monotonous activities and enhances human work.

- The Job Market and Automation: AI will undoubtedly replace certain occupations, but it will also open up new career prospects. People could be freed from risky or repetitive jobs by automation, freeing them up to concentrate on strategic, creative, or social duties. Making sure that people have the skills necessary to prosper in this new economy will be a problem.

- Economic redistribution and universal basic income: Governments may need to take into account alternate models for economic support, such universal basic income (UBI), as AI-driven automation lessens the necessity for traditional jobs. In an economy where many jobs are automated, universal basic income (UBI) would ensure that everyone may benefit from the prosperity brought about by AI.

Social Organizations and Governance in Societies Driven by AI

The emergence of AI will also change societal institutions and government. The obstacles presented by AI, such as concerns about data security, privacy, and moral decision-making, may require traditional political institutions to change.

- AI in Governance: By facilitating data-driven policy implementation, more effective decision-making, and individualized services for citizens, AI has the potential to completely transform governance. This, however, brings up issues with data privacy, surveillance, and the consolidation of power in the hands of a small number of governments or tech firms.

- Inclusion and Social Equity: Making sure that the advantages of AI are distributed fairly will be essential as it grows more and more integrated into society. Because individuals who have access to AI technology enjoy a disproportionate advantage, there is a chance that AI will worsen already-existing inequities. It is important to make sure that everyone may take advantage of the developments in AI, irrespective of their socioeconomic background.

9.4 Getting Ready for the Unknown: Adaptability, Foresight, and Resilience

It is impossible to foresee exactly how artificial intelligence will develop in the future. However, by encouraging foresight, adaptability, and resilience in both people and institutions, we can get ready for the future. These characteristics will be crucial for negotiating the impending rapid technological developments.

Developing Resilience in People and Organizations

One essential quality that will assist people and organizations in navigating the uncertain terrain of AI advancement is resilience, or the capacity to adjust and flourish in the face of change. Adapting to new tools, processes, and social norms will be crucial in a world where technology advancements are happening at an accelerated rate.

- Lifelong Learning: The skills needed for success will change as AI changes industries. People will need to continuously improve their expertise in order to be relevant in the workforce, making lifelong learning crucial. Online courses, mentorship programs, and flexible educational systems that prioritize flexibility and critical thinking can all help achieve this.

Encouraging Adaptability and Flexibility

Institutions and individuals alike must continue to be flexible and adaptable due to the rapid rate of technological change. This adaptability will be essential for both accepting AI and handling any unexpected repercussions or moral conundrums it may raise.

- Institutional Flexibility: Systems must be made flexible by governments, corporations, and educational institutions. This could entail developing innovative ecosystems that promote experimentation and adaptability, implementing decentralized organizational structures, and developing flexible policy frameworks.

Strategic planning and foresight

Even though AI's future is unpredictable, strategic foresight can assist direct choices and actions now. People and organizations can create backup plans and get ready for a range of futures by foreseeing possible situations and results.

- Scenario Planning: This process entails examining a variety of potential scenarios and formulating plans for each. From extremely cooperative AI ecosystems to situations where AI development causes major societal upheaval, this can assist enterprises in preparing for the various and uncertain ways that AI may develop.

There are a lot of opportunities and difficulties associated with the future of intelligence and autonomy. We can build a future in which humans and AI coexist by comprehending the evolutionary continuum between humans and AI, investigating the potential for emergent sentience, and becoming ready for societal and economic changes. Resilience and flexibility will be crucial and moral insight, guaranteeing that AI stays an aid for human well-being rather than a disruptive force.

CHAPTER 10

CONCLUSION: INTELLIGENCE-BASED EMPOWERMENT

Exploring the significant and revolutionary effects that agentic AI is expected to have on society has been the quest of this book. We have looked at how AI could change every aspect of our life, from comprehending the changing human-AI interaction to addressing the existential and ethical issues these technologies bring up. By highlighting the significance of human agency in the creation and use of AI and outlining a positive, moral course for the future, this last chapter seeks to synthesize these findings.

10.1 Integrating the Agentic Framework

In summary, agentic AI describes systems that are active agents with the ability to behave autonomously, make decisions, and adapt to complicated contexts rather than merely being passive tools. These systems can reason, learn, and adapt in ways that resemble human decision-making processes; they are not just made to carry out commands. The autonomy of agentic AI is what makes it so potent; it can function without direct human input, completing jobs and solving issues in real time with amazing creativity and efficiency.

The Potential Benefits of Agentic AI

Agentic AI's capabilities create previously unheard-of opportunities in a number of fields:

- Autonomous Problem Solving: Agentic AI can be used in limited or unrealistic human intervention scenarios. In the healthcare industry, for instance, autonomous systems can evaluate medical data and suggest therapies without continual oversight, freeing up physicians to concentrate on more complicated patient needs.

- Adaptation in Real-Time: These systems are always learning and changing. They are therefore perfect for applications such as financial forecasting, supply chain management, and climate change modeling since they can improve operations in real-time.

- Human-Machine Collaboration: Agentic AI enhances human capabilities rather than taking the place of them. AI can collaborate with people to address activities that call for both human intuition and machine efficiency, from creative domains like music and art to engineering and scientific research.

The Significance of It

The development of agentic AI signifies a paradigm shift in our understanding of intelligence, labor, and human potential rather than merely a technical advancement. Because of these technologies' tremendous capabilities, we are forced to face new ethical and societal impact concerns. Whether these technologies enhance mankind or become a source of inequality and divide depends on how we decide to develop, govern, and integrate them.

- It's important to keep in mind the core idea of this book as we go into an AI-enhanced world: human agency remains at the center of the AI equation.

Agentic AI is a tool designed by humans to be influenced and guided by human values, ethics, and objectives; it is not an independent force in and of itself.

10.2 Looping Human Agency

Although agentic AI has a lot of potential, how humans choose to use it will determine how powerful it is. This book's premise of human agency and the deliberate control humans have over the technology we develop is among its most significant revelations.

Human Intention's Enduring Value

The importance of human intention cannot be overstated, even in a time when machines are becoming more autonomous. Although AI systems can absorb information and make judgments, their purpose is determined by human vision, values, and ethical considerations. To put it another way, we need to make sure AI stays in line with human objectives and aspirations. How we use these technologies will ultimately depend on the decisions we make regarding their creation, application, and regulation.

Think about the healthcare industry once more. Although AI-powered diagnostic tools are incredibly effective, they must be directed by human empathy and a knowledge of each patient's particular needs. Without human supervision, AI may emphasize efficiency above empathy or fall victim to algorithmic biases. We can make sure AI fulfills its full potential by carefully combining human knowledge with machine intelligence.

Vision and Empathy: The Human Touch

Although agentic AI is capable of task execution, outcome prediction, and system optimization, it lacks empathy, vision, and the complex comprehension of human experience. These uniquely human characteristics are what make our technologies work. While vision motivates us to develop AI systems that promote development, equity, and constructive societal transformation, empathy enables us to take into account the social, cultural, and psychological effects of AI.

For this reason, it's crucial that humans stay in the loop, particularly about the moral ramifications of AI. Human oversight guarantees that AI stays a positive force, regardless of whether we are discussing data privacy, AI prejudice, or the economic displacement of workers. We need to be proactive and watchful to ensure that AI is built with our core values such as justice, fairness, and respect for human dignity in mind.

10.3 Outlining the Way Ahead

The incorporation of AI into society offers both urgent issues and fascinating opportunities as we move to the future. In the next stage of AI research, ethical frameworks, inclusion, and the pursuit of innovation that benefits everyone must be carefully considered.

Ethical Innovation: Establishing Structures for Conscientious AI Creation

We must create strong ethical standards that can direct the development and application of AI if we want it to benefit humanity in a way that respects our values and interests.

These rules ought to cover issues like:

- Transparency: Making sure AI systems are accountable and comprehensible. Developers should be able to disclose the data and procedures that AI systems use to make judgments, as well as explain how these decisions are made.

- The design of AI systems must avoid prejudice in order to ensure that they are equitable and do not reinforce or worsen societal disparities. Diversifying the data sets used to train AI and regularly checking systems for fairness are necessary to achieve this.

- Accountability: As AI grows more independent, accountability concerns surface. When an AI system errs or hurts people, who is responsible? To guarantee that AI developers and users are held accountable for the activities of their systems, institutional and legal frameworks must be put in place.

- Sustainability: We must take the environment into

account when creating AI technologies. The development of AI should be in line with more general sustainability objectives, from energy usage to the moral sourcing of resources.

Inclusivity: Guaranteeing Widespread Involvement in the AI Revolution

AI needs to be inclusive if it is to be genuinely transformative. This entails making sure that different voices and viewpoints are included in the creation of AI in addition to making sure that its advantages are widely shared throughout society. All too frequently, a small number of stakeholders dictate technology advancements, resulting in systems that only represent a small variety of demands and experiences.

Development of inclusive AI can be accomplished by:

In order to ensure that the AI systems we develop are more representative of the diverse world we live in, it is important to promote diversity in the tech sector, particularly among women, minorities, and underrepresented groups.

- Ensuring Access to AI: Not everyone should be able to take use of AI's advantages. The digital divide can be closed and more egalitarian possibilities can be created for everyone if AI technologies are made available to everyone, regardless of location, socioeconomic background, or level of education.

- International Cooperation: AI is a global phenomenon, and its opportunities and difficulties are felt globally. Establishing shared ethical norms and making sure AI research is safe and advantageous for all people, regardless of state borders, require international cooperation.

Innovation That Transforms: Going Beyond Efficiency

The true transformational potential of AI resides in its capacity to solve issues that humans have never been able to solve before, even though a large portion of the discussion surrounding AI has been on increasing efficiency and optimizing current systems. AI has the capacity to solve some of the most important issues facing the world today, from halting climate change to improving medical research.

Beyond efficiency, we need to promote innovation if we are to realize AI's full potential. We may map out a future in which artificial intelligence (AI) transforms into a transformative tool for sustainability, equity, and progress by concentrating on finding solutions to major problems and opening up new avenues for human flourishing.

10.4 Concluding Thoughts: Working Together to Build a Future Worth Living In

It is crucial that we leave our exploration of the realm of agentic AI with a vision of what might be in the future—a future in which AI and people co-create a better world for everybody. In order to realize this goal, we must envision a world in which we collaborate with machines to create something bigger than ourselves, rather than merely having machines work for us.

This is a challenge to our shared creativity and

accountability, not a utopian ideal. The decisions we make today will influence the direction of AI in the future. Will we let AI separate us, make inequality worse, or take over our lives in ways we can't control? Or will we decide to create a future in which AI supports human growth by boosting our potential for empathy, creativity, and group action?

Let's remember the timeless strength of human agency as we enter this new era the ability to direct, influence, and co-create the future we desire. We have the chance to create AI systems that respect and elevate the principles that make us human while simultaneously advancing technological advancement. This is our time's chance and struggle.

By working together, we can create a future in which AI and people coexist peacefully, enabling us to address the major issues of our day and create a world that future generations will want to live in.

ABOUT THE AUTHOR

 Jaxon Vale, who specializes in AI-driven tactics that enable people to create scalable enterprises, is an ardent supporter of the nexus between technology and entrepreneurship. Jaxon has been in the vanguard of using artificial intelligence for creative and commercial endeavors, having a background in digital transformation, data science, and machine learning.

Jaxon has offered advice on how to use AI to advance oneself, make money from digital abilities, and expand side projects into successful companies over the years. Jaxon has worked with innumerable budding entrepreneurs, offering them tools, methods, and tips for success in the digital age. He has a natural curiosity and a dedication to helping others achieve.

When not working in the fields of artificial intelligence and business development, Jaxon likes to experiment with new technologies, produce creative digital content, and coach people on how to succeed in the rapidly evolving world of tech-driven opportunities.